The Condon Gang

The Chicago and New York Jazz Scene

TROMBONE

MUSIC MINUS ONE

SUGGESTIONS FOR USING THIS MMO EDITION

WE HAVE TRIED to create a product that will provide you an easy way to learn and perform these jazz classics with a complete accompaniment in the comfort of your own home. Because it involves a fixed accompaniment, there is an inherent lack of flexibility in tempo. The following MMO features and techniques will reduce these inflexibilities and help you maximize the effectiveness of the MMO practice and performance system:

We have observed generally accepted tempi, but some may wish to perform at a different tempo, or to slow down or speed up the accompaniment for practice purposes. Though we have provided several of the most up-tempo tunes on this album at a -20% speed for your practice usage, you can also purchase from MMO specialized CD players and recorders which allow continu-ously variable speed while maintaining proper pitch. This is an indispensable tool for the serious musician and you may wish to look into purchasing this useful piece of equipment for full enjoyment of all your MMO editions.

Where the performer begins a piece *solo* or without an introduction from the accompanying ensemble, we have provided a set of subtle taps before each piece as appropriate to help you enter with the proper tempo.

We want to provide you with the most useful practice and performance accompaniments possible. If you have any suggestions for improving the MMO system, please feel free to contact us. You can reach us by e-mail at *mmogroup@musicminusone.com*.

NOTES TO THE PERFORMER

WHEN A JAZZ MUSICIAN LEARNS A SONG he/she tries to go to the source (sometimes the original sheet music or sometimes a famous recording of that song). In this way the musician has a good understanding of what the composer intended. From here the performer can interpret the song in his/her own style. When you listen to these songs and follow along with the music you will not hear the exact notes written on the page. You will see the music that was sourced from original sheet music but hear the musicians' improvised interpretation of that melody. To play the melodies exactly as written would make the tune sound stiff and contrived, but to transcribe exactly what is played here by these musicians would look extremely complicated on the manuscript. This is the nature of jazz. It is an aural art form and is learned by listening, copying and inventing. Try to "play around" with the melody when you play with the band. You can even use your interpretation of the melody when it's your turn to solo. If you are not sure what to do, listen to your instrument on the complete version of the CD. Maybe you can try to copy him/her. You might also like to find other recordings of these songs and listen to how the performer stylizes the song.

All songs in this style of jazz have what is known as a "form". Many songs have a 32-bar form (e.g. *Monday Date* is A, A, B, A or *The One I Love Belongs To Somebody Else* is A, B, A, C). Some have Verse, Chorus (*Skeleton Jangle* – where you stay on the chorus for solos) and some just have a set number of bars (*Georgia Grind* – 12 bar blues). It is very important to know the form of a song, as this is what helps you keep your place within the performance of that song. If you look at the concert lead sheets in this book you will see the form of the song (melody and chords from beginning to end) and the routines that were used for this recording. If you are having difficulty keeping your place during solos of other instruments then sing the melody in your head (or hum softly) to help yourself keep place. Of course you can just count the amount of bars you must rest (or accompany for piano/ drums), but "knowing" where you are in a song because of the harmonic changes is extremely important in playing jazz.

Each instrument has a certain role to play in a jazz band. In this recording you will hear different instruments taking the lead, soloing, accompanying and also making rhythmic punctuation. Listen carefully to the role that your instrument plays. You will hear that it may change at times, sometimes playing collective improvisation, sometimes taking the lead, accompanying or soloing. If you are ever in doubt as to what to play, listen to the complete-version CD again and pick out what your instrument is doing at that particular point.

Most importantly, have fun. Turn your player up loud and blow to your heart's content!

—*Anita Thomas*

3923

CONTENTS

Monday Date

by Earl Hines

1st X Piano Solo (Trombone Tacet)
2nd X Ad Lib Ensemble – Trumpet Lead

Ensemble Explosion

The One I Love Belongs To Somebody Else

by Isham Jones
& Gus Kahn

MMO 3923

Strut Miss Lizzie

by Henry Creamer
& Turner Layton

MMO 3923

TROMBONE IN 𝄢

Georgia Grind

By Spencer Williams

Trombone in 𝄢

SKELETON JANGLE

by Edwin B. Edwards,
D. James LaRocca, Henry Ragas,
Anthony Sbarbaro and Larry Shields

A KISS TO BUILD A DREAM ON

By Bert Kalmar, Harry Ruby
& Oscar Hammerstein II

I Know That You Know

by Anne Caldwell
and Vincent Youmans

MMO 3923

TROMBONE IN 𝄢

I Must Have That Man

By Dorothy Fields & Jimmy McHugh

TROMBONE IN 𝄢

Jazz Me Blues

by Tom Delaney

CONCERT LEAD SHEET

Monday Date

by Earl Hines

4 Bar Solo Piano Intro
Piano Lead 1 Chorus (Tacet Horns)
   (Ensemble explosion)
Ensemble - Trumpet Lead 1 Chorus
Trombone Solo 16 Bars / Clarinet Solo 16 Bars
Tenor Sax Solo 16 Bars / Trumpet Solo 16 Bars
Piano Solo 1 Chorus
Ensemble - Trumpet Lead 1 Chorus (Bass Solo on Bridge)
4 Bar Solo Piano Tag
4 Bar Ensemble Tag - Trumpet Lead

MMO 3923

The One I Love Belongs To Somebody Else

Last 8 Bars Ensemble Intro – Trumpet Lead
Trombone Solo Lead 1 Chorus
Ensemble – Trumpet Lead 1 Chorus
Piano Solo 16 Bars / Trumpet Solo 16 Bars
Tenor Sax Solo 16 Bars / Guitar Solo 16 Bars
Clarinet Solo 24 Bars (Ensemble Backing)
8 Bars Ensemble Ending – Trumpet Lead

by Isham Jones
& Gus Kahn

MMO 3923

Strut Miss Lizzie

by Henry Creamer
& Turner Layton

Last 8 Bars Ensemble Intro – Trumpet Lead
Ensemble – Trumpet Lead 1 Chorus
Piano Solo 1 Chorus (Ensemble explosion)
Trumpet Solo 1 Chorus (Ensemble Explosion)
Tenor Sax Solo 1 Chorus (Ensemble Explosion)
Trombone Solo 1 Chorus (Ensemble Explosion)
Clarinet Solo 1 Chorus (Ensemble Backing / Ensemble Explosion)
Ensemble – Trumpet Lead 1 Chorus (Stop And Go / Flare)
Ensemble – Trumpet Lead 1 Chorus
4 Bar Solo Drum Tag
4 Bar Ensemble Tag – Trumpet Lead

CONCERT LEAD SHEET

Georgia Grind

By Spencer Williams

4 Bar Solo Piano Intro
Ensemble - Trumpet Lead 1 Chorus
Clarinet Solo 2 Choruses (1st chorus with 3 beat rhythm)
Trombone Solo 1 Chorus
Tenor Sax Solo 1 Chorus
Trumpet Solo 1 Chorus
Piano Solo 1 Chorus
Guitar Solo 1 Chorus
Bass Solo 1 Chorus
Ensemble - Trumpet Lead 2 Choruses
   (Clarinet Break / Ensemble End - Trumpet Lead)

MMO 3923

CONCERT LEAD SHEET

ENSEMBLE – TRUMPET LEAD – VERSE AND CHORUS
TROMBONE SOLO 1 CHORUS (ENSEMBLE EXPLOSION)
TRUMPET SOLO 1 CHORUS (ENSEMBLE EXPLOSION)
TENOR SAX SOLO 1 CHORUS (ENSEMBLE EXPLOSION)
CLARINET SOLO 1 CHORUS (ENSEMBLE EXPLOSION)
PIANO SOLO 1 CHORUS
ENSEMBLE – TRUMPET LEAD – VERSE AND CHORUS (WITH STOP AND GO)
ENSEMBLE – TRUMPET LEAD – 1 CHORUS
4 BAR SOLO CLARINET TAG
4 BAR ENSEMBLE TAG – TRUMPET LEAD

SKELETON JANGLE

by Edwin B. Edwards,
D. James LaRocca, Henry Ragas,
Anthony Sbarbaro and Larry Shields

CONCERT LEAD SHEET

4 Bar Solo Trumpet Intro
Trumpet Solo Lead 1 Chorus (Horns Back Up on Bridge)
Vocal Chorus (Clarinet / Tenor Sax Backing)
Trombone Solo 8 Bars / Clarinet Solo 8 Bars
Guitar Solo 8 Bars / Tenor Sax Solo 8 Bars
Piano Solo 16 Bars
Trumpet Solo 8 Bars Bridge (Horns Back Up)
8 Bars Ensemble - Trumpet Lead - Ending

A KISS TO BUILD A DREAM ON

By Bert Kalmar, Harry Ruby
& Oscar Hammerstein II

MMO 3923

CONCERT LEAD SHEET

8 Bar Solo Drum Intro
Ensemble - Trumpet Lead 1 Chorus
Clarinet Solo 1 Chorus
Piano Solo 1 Chorus
Trumpet Solo 1 Chorus
Drum Solo 1 Chorus (Ensemble Stops)
Ensemble - Trumpet Lead 1 Chorus - Ending

I Know That You Know

by Anne Caldwell
and Vincent Youmans

MMO 3923

I Must Have That Man

4 Bar Solo Tenor Sax Intro
Tenor Sax Solo Lead 1 Chorus (Ensemble Backing On Bridge)
Trumpet Solo 16 Bars / Trombone Solo 16 Bars
Piano Solo 16 Bars / Clarinet Solo 16 Bars
Tenor Sax Solo 16 Bars (Ensemble Backing)
Ensemble 16 Bars - Trumpet Lead - Ending

By Dorothy Fields & Jimmy McHugh

MMO 3923

CONCERT LEAD SHEET

ENSEMBLE VERSE - TRUMPET LEAD (1ST X CLARINET BREAK / 2ND X TRUMPET BREAK)
ENSEMBLE INTERLUDE & CHORUS - TRUMPET LEAD
CLARINET SOLO 1 CHORUS
TENOR SAX SOLO 1 CHORUS
TRUMPET SOLO 1 CHORUS
TROMBONE SOLO 1 CHORUS
PIANO SOLO 1 CHORUS
ENSEMBLE VERSE - TRUMPET LEAD (1ST X TROMBONE BREAK / 2ND X BASS BREAK)
ENSEMBLE INTERLUDE & CHORUS - TRUMPET LEAD (STOP AND GO / FLARE)
ENSEMBLE CHORUS - TRUMPET LEAD
4 BAR SOLO DRUM TAG
4 BAR ENSEMBLE TAG - TRUMPET LEAD

JAZZ ME BLUES

by Tom Delaney

MMO 3923

THE PERFORMERS

CHRIS TYLE (cornet, vocal) Chris, a native of Portland, Oregon, discovered hot jazz in the record collection of his father, Axel—the original drummer with Portland's Castle Jazz Band. Naturally, Chris started his musical career as a drummer, but took up cornet in the mid-1970s. He played around Portland with Don Kinch's Conductors, the Rose City Jazz Band, Jim Beatty's Jazz Band and others until moving to the Bay Area and a job with Turk Murphy in 1979. Later, upon his return to Portland, Chris organized a swing quartet called Wholly Cats, featuring top jazz vocalist Rebecca Kilgore. In the '80s Chris returned to the drums and worked steadily with Stumptown Jazz. At the end of the decade he moved to New Orleans, where he played with Danny Barker, Banu Gibson, the Mahogany Hall Stompers, Creole Rice Jazz Band and co-led the Frisco Syncopators with Hal Smith. In 1992 Chris organized the Silver Leaf Jazz Band. This group performed six nights a week for 10 years at the Can Can Jazz Café on Bourbon Street and recorded musical tributes to King Oliver, Freddie Keppard, Jelly Roll Morton and New Orleans Composers for the **Good Time Jazz** and **Stomp Off** labels. During this time, Chris taught himself to play clarinet and wound up playing cornet, clarinet and drums on jobs in New Orleans. He recorded as a drummer with bands led by Duke Heitger and Tommy Sancton and on clarinet with Andrew Hall. When the Can Can engagement ended, Chris returned to Portland. He has since reorganized the Silver Leaf Jazz Band and also works with the Riverboat Jazz Band, in addition to tours with the Ophelia Ragtime Orchestra, Orange Kellin Trio and others. Chris' favorite cornetists/trumpeters include Louis Armstrong, King Oliver, Freddie Keppard, Bunk Johnson, Bix Beiderbecke, Henry Red Allen, Rex Stewart, Wild Bill Davison and Max Kaminsky. Chris has been one of the cornet instructors at the Adult Traditional Jazz Camp in San Diego, presented each January by America's Finest City Dixieland Jazz Society.

CLINT BAKER (trombone) As a teenager in the Bay Area, Clint played with a youth group called "Greasy Kid Stuff." He started out playing drums and tuba, then became proficient on trumpet, trombone, clarinet, sax, banjo, guitar and string bass. While in his 20s Clint worked with the Zenith Jazz Band, Good Time Levee Stompers, Magnolia Jazz Band, New Orleans Wanderers and the San Francisco Legacy. In 1987 he organized Clint Baker's New Orleans Jazz Band, which was popular on the West Coast jazz festival circuit and also appeared in Canada and at the New Orleans Jazz &Heritage Festival. Between 1987 and the present, Clint has played the instruments listed above with such bands as the Boilermaker Jazz Band, Roadrunners, Tom Sharpsteen's Orlandos, Elysian Fields Orchestra, Imperial Serenaders, Black Diamond Blue Five, Mal Sharpe's Big Money In Dixieland band and groups led by George Probert, Big Bill Bissonnette and Bill Carter. More recently, Clint has worked with the Jim Cullum Jazz Band, Climax Jazz Band, Port City Jazz Band, Grand Dominion Jazz Band, Gremoli and the Vancouver Classic Jazz Band. He has also reorganized the New Orleans Jazz Band. Besides that group, Clint leads the Café Borrone All Stars, who have appeared regularly for 13 years at Café Borrone in Menlo Park, California. Clint is also a regular with the Yerba Buena Stompers and Leon Oakley's Friends of Jazz Band. He gives private lessons and lectures on jazz history to Elderhostel groups. He has taught trumpet, banjo, guitar, tuba and bass at the AFCDJS Adult Traditional Jazz Camp. Among Clint's influences on trombone: Kid Ory, J.C. Higginbotham, Dickie Wells, Bob Mielke, Bill Bardin.

BOBBY GORDON (clarinet) Bobby studied with Chicago clarinetist Joe Marsala and played sessions with Pee Wee Russell in New York. He did a stint with Muggsy Spanier and also played with Condon alumni Bobby Hackett, Wild Bill Davison and Condon himself. In the '60s Bobby recorded several albums with strings for **Decca**. These sessions are eagerly sought by collectors. He nearly became a member of Louis Armstrong's All Stars, but Armstrong's ill health forced the group to disband before Bobby could join. A similar set of circumstances prevented Bobby from becoming the clarinetist with Bob Scobey's band in Chicago. Nevertheless, Bobby worked around Chicago before moving to San Antonio and a job with the Jim Cullum Jazz Band. Later, Bobby toured with pop star Leon Redbone and appeared with him on Johnny Carson's *Tonight Show*. Since relocating to San Diego, Bobby has worked with many local bands and led his own group for a long run at Milligan's in La Jolla. He has performed at venues across the U.S. and has toured overseas in Europe and Japan. Bobby has recorded extensively with guitarist/vocalist Marty Grosz, with the Roadrunners (including vocalist Rebecca Kilgore) and under his own name on the **Arbors** label. Bobby continues to play jazz parties and festivals as a guest artist and leads both a trio and sextet for jobs on the West Coast. It is easy to hear Joe Marsala's tremendous influence on Bobby, though he has also been inspired by Pee Wee Russell, Jimmie Noone, Jimmy Dorsey and Frank Teschemacher.

ANITA THOMAS (tenor sax) was raised in a music-loving environment in Australia. As a youth, she studied guitar, then flute and clarinet. Later she entered the Sydney Conservatorium of Music High School and took up piano. Anita attended Pan Pacific Jazz Camps for many years, beginning in 1983. During this time she organized a quartet with her bass-playing sister Natalie. She had become proficient on various saxophones and the combo performed on tv, radio and at concerts in the Sydney area. In 1989, Anita completed the Associate Diploma of Jazz Studies as an arranging major. She played in the orchestra for musical productions of "42nd Street" and "Cabaret". For many years she was an instructor for Pan Pacific at both junior and adult camps and in 1996, she became the musical director of the Pan Pacific Jazz Camp. Anita played frequently alongside sister Natalie with virtuoso multi-instrumentalist James Morrison and also in John Morrison's "Swing City" Big Band. She also recorded for many Australian artists in jazz, pop and rock and for 6 years was the co-host of a weekly jazz radio program in Sydney. Since 1994 Anita had her own jazz group that played at festivals and concerts throughout Australia. The band recorded a CD in 1998 and a second in 2001. Soon after, Anita and her husband relocated to the Greater Los Angeles area. In Southern California, Anita has played all kinds of jazz from New Orleans to Bop and beyond. She is a regular with the Reynolds Brothers Rhythm Rascals, Baldy Mountain Swing and Hal's Angels. She has also worked with the Golden Eagle Jazz Band, Bobby Gordon Sextet, Café Borrone All Stars, Firehouse Stompers, Jazz Chihuahuas, the Tim Davies Big Band and the Clayton-Hamilton Jazz Orchestra. Besides her considerable talents as a reed player and arranger, Anita is a terrific vocalist, acoustic rhythm guitarist and bassist.

MMO 3923

RAY SKJELBRED (piano) Ray, a Chicago native, is one of the best practitioners of that city's piano tradition. He is an enthusiastic fan of Frank Melrose, George Zack, Alex Hill, William Barbee, Zinky Cohn and Cassino Simpson. and became acquainted with Earl Hines, Joe Sullivan, Jess Stacy and Art Hodes while living on the West Coat. As a young man, Ray lived in Seattle, where he studied with pianist Johnny Wittwer. On trips to the Bay Area, he also heard the great Burt Bales, who became another major influence. Together with Seattle bassist Mike Duffy, Ray co-led the Great Excelsior Jazz Band. The GEJB recorded with vocalist Claire Austin and cornetist Jim Goodwin. Ray also played with Monte Ballou (leader of the Castle Jazz Band). In 1969 Ray relocated to the Bay Area. In short order he became the leading traditional jazz pianist in the area, playing solo jobs and working with the Jelly Roll Jazz Band, Bay City Jazz Band, Bob Mielke's Bearcats, New Orleans Jazz Club of Northern California All Stars, the Golden Age Jazz Band and others. He led a swing band called Berkeley Rhythm and played a long residency at the Bull Valley Inn in Port Costa, where the Bay Area's best jazz musicians came to jam. In addition, he played trombone with several groups. Ray's career as an English teacher was put on hold when he joined Turk Murphy's Jazz Band in 1983, staying for three years. After leaving Murphy, he resumed teaching, though continuing to play as often as his schedule permitted. He recorded with the Bobby Gordon Trio and the San Francisco-style Down Home Jazz Band and with the late Barbara Lashley, a superb vocalist. In the 1990s he was a regular with the Roadrunners—featuring Rebecca Kilgore, Bobby Gordon and Hal Smith. In the recent past, he has appeared with Barbara Dane's Goodtime Bonanza Band, the Usonia Six, Bob Schulz's Frisco Jazz Band, Leon Oakley's Friends of Jazz, the Port City Jazz Band and his own "Monogram Boys" and "Yeti Chasers." His recent quartet CD features Katie Cavera, Clint Baker and Hal Smith.

MARTY EGGERS (bass) Started his musical career as a ragtime pianist. In the early '80s he began listening to live jazz, played by Turk Murphy, the Golden Eagles, Tom Sharpsteen and others. He organized the "Front Street Wanderers" in high school and was involved in the formation of the Sacramento Ragtime Society. He joined the Black Diamond Blue Five on piano and while in college he worked with a 10-piece dance band called the "California Blues Destroyers." Marty tried playing cornet, but did not stay with the instrument. After graduation, with an engineering degree, Marty took a job as a software engineer. He became a full-time musician in 1991 after being laid off from the engineering job. Marty had been interested in string bass for a long time when he happened to try out Clint Baker's bass during a visit. Before long he was playing bass with Jerry Kaehle's Good Time Levee Stompers. Marty became the bassist with "Bo Grumpus" in 1991. The trio performed across the U.S. and made several recordings during its 11 years of activity. In addition to his work with Bo Grumpus, Marty continued to play with the Black Diamond Blue Five, plus Clint Baker's New Orleans Jazz Band and the Roadrunners. He recorded three CDs with Chris Tyle's Silver Leaf Jazz Band and two with the California Swing Cats, featuring Rebecca Kilgore and Tim Laughlin. This group toured Europe twice. In 1997 he joined the Butch Thompson Trio on bass. Marty is married to ragtime pianist Virginia Tichenor. They play together in the "Tichenor Family Trio," which includes Virginia's father Trebor (a renowned ragtime scholar). Marty's other musical affiliations at the present time include the Yerba Buena Stompers (piano), the Carl Sonny Leyland Trio (bass) and a solo piano job at Pier 23 in San Francisco, where Burt Bales was the soloist in the '50s and '60s. Marty also edits the *Frisco Cricket*, the publication of the San Francisco Traditional Jazz Foundation. His favorite bassist is New Orleanian Bill Johnson.

KATIE CAVERA (guitar) Katie studied with Dr. David Baker at Indiana University and was the banjoist with Baker's Orchestra, performing at the Smithsonian Institution's Duke Ellington Festival. Katie composed and arranged music for many IU theatrical productions including "Sweet Bird of Youth" and "Taming of the Shrew." She moved to California and became involved in the Southern California jazz scene, working with George Probert, The Crazy Rhythm Hot Society and others. Katie studied banjo with John Reynolds and Eddie Erickson. In 2000, she took Rebecca Kilgore's guitar class at the AFCDJS Swing Camp. During the weekend she was introduced to instructors Clint Baker and Hal Smith. Katie proved to be one of the star pupils of the Swing Camp and repeated the performance on banjo a year later at the Traditional Jazz Camp. Following the 2001 Trad Camp, Katie was hired as an instructor. Katie is now one of the busiest banjoists and guitarists on the West Coast. Her band credits include work with the Roadrunners, Elysian Fields Orchestra, George Probert's Monrovia Old Style Jazz Band, the Crazy Rhythm Hot Society Orchestra, Golden Eagle Jazz Band and a trip to San Antonio to work with Jim Cullum's Jazz Band. Besides these groups, Katie is a regular with the Firehouse Stompers, CJ and Katie, Clint Baker's New Orleans Jazz Band, Usonia Jazz, Hal's Angels, the New Orleans Wanderers and Jazz Chihuahuas. In addition to her work on banjo and guitar, Katie is a fine vocalist, arranger and string bassist. She is also a talented actress, having appeared with her husband (magician Woody Pittman) in the short film "Blood Day." Recently, Katie and Anita Thomas acted in and played music for Woody's special "Magic-O-Rama" presentation. Her favorite guitarists include Freddie Green, Allan Reuss, Steve Jordan and George Van Eps.

HAL SMITH (drums, leader) Hal took up drums in 1963. He was inspired by hearing Ben Pollack, Nick Fatool, Fred Higuera, Smokey Stover, Wayne Jones and others in person. In the '70s he began to study recordings by classic jazz drummers, to learn all the vintage jazz drum styles. Hal played with a Dixieland band in high school and sat in with Turk Murphy's Jazz Band and the South Frisco Jazz Band. Later, at college, he studied journalism rather than music. After graduating with a B.A. in 1976, Hal attempted to work as a newspaperman, but wound up as a printer. In 1978 he gave up printing to work as a full-time musician. He has worked with the Dukes of Dixieland, Wilber/Davern Summit Reunion, Jim Cullum's Jazz Band, Lawson-Haggart Jazz Band, Climax Jazz Band, Salty Dogs, Silver Leaf Jazz Band, Grand Dominion Jazz Band, Chicago Rhythm, Tim Laughlin, Marty Grosz, Golden State Jazz Band, Hall Brothers Jazz Band, Golden Eagle Jazz Band, Clint Baker's New Orleans Jazz Band and individuals from Bud Freeman to Scott Hamilton. The Roadrunners, Creole Sunshine Jazz Band, Down Home Jazz Band, Frisco Syncopators and the California Swing Cats are some of the bands Hal led in the past. Currently he works with Bob Schulz's Frisco Jazz Band, Alan Adams' New Orleans Wanderers, the Carl Sonny Leyland Trio, the Bobby Gordon Sextet, Leon Oakley's Friends of Jazz Band and the Butch Thompson Trio. He leads "Hal's Angels" and also the "Jazz Chihuahuas" which includes his wife June on acoustic guitar. Hal has made over 150 recording sessions. He is Administrative and Media Director of AFCDJS-San Diego and is the faculty drum instructor at the AFCDJS Adult Jazz Camp. He is a contributing writer to *Mississippi Rag*, *American Rag*, *Jazz Rambler*, *Frisco Cricket*, *Just Jazz* (Great Britain) and the *Bulletin of the Hot Club of France*. Besides the drummers named earlier, Hal's favorites include Sid Catlett, Jo Jones, Dave Tough, Zutty Singleton, Baby Dodds and Ray Bauduc.

MUSIC MINUS ONE

50 Executive Boulevard ⬩ Elmsford, New York 10523-1325
1.800.669.7464 U.S. ⬩ 914.592.1188 International
www.musicminusone.com ⬩ mmogroup@musicminusone.com